The Humble Assessment

A PLAY

IN

THREE ACTS

OF

DESPERATION

BY KRIS SAKNUSSEMM

With a foreword by Phil Abrams
and an afterword by the Author

A LAZY FASCIST BOOK

Lazy Fascist Press
an imprint of Eraserhead Press
205 NE Bryant Street
Portland, Oregon 97211

www.lazyfascistpress.com

ISBN: 978-1-62105-081-0

Copyright © 2013 by Kris Saknussemm

Cover art copyright © 2013 by Matthew Revert

Cover design by Matthew Revert
www.matthewrevert.com

An earlier version of this work was first performed at the Victorian College of the Arts, Melbourne Australia, April 2010.

All rights reserved. No part of this book may be reproduced or transmitted in any form or by any means, electronic or mechanical, including photocopying, recording, or by any information storage and retrieval system, without the written consent of the publisher, except where permitted by law.

Printed in the USA.

PRAISE FOR KRIS SAKNUSSEMM

"James Ellroy meets David Lynch."
—PUBLISHERS WEEKLY

"Kris Saknussemm's sincerity, wisdom, and writing talent make *Sea Monkeys* something which is half way between a memoir and a Molotov cocktail."
—ETGAR KERET

"Kris Saknussemm is a brilliant writer."
—MICHAEL MOORCOCK

"Kris Saknussemm has a voice like no one else's."
—JOAN WICKERSHAM, National Book Award finalist

"Saknussemm is a rare visionary of American culture, a fearless artist with his very own skew on the western world. *Reverend America* is brilliant!"
—JONATHAN EVISON, *New York Times* bestselling author of *West of Here*

"One is hard pressed, while reading him, to recall the existence of any other reality."
—THE BOSTON REVIEW

"...an original blend of noir procedural, horror, and dark eroticism."
—SCHOOL LIBRARY JOURNAL

"*Enigmatic Pilot* is a rip-roaring trip through a fantastic mid-19th century America...written in the spirit of Mark Twain's novelistic journeys."
—THE WALL STREET JOURNAL

"It is the remarkable intermingling of the communicative and defensive aspects of speech which characterizes every interview."

—Otto Allen Will, Jr.

FOREWORD BY PHIL ABRAMS

INSTRUCTIONS FOR READING THE HUMBLE ASSESSMENT:

1) Take a deep breath. 2) Shudder as the stark images and truth of the narrative sink in and swirl around your psyche.

At once, names like Ionesco, Beckett, and Albee come to mind, but then are topped by the understanding that this voice has an even more unsettling, hard-hitting edge. As you reach the epilogue, Kris Saknussemm plunges, then twists his theatrical knife deep into your heart—deeper than you can imagine or necessarily want! Like a cat o' nine tails working you over, your flesh is raw, exposed, and ready to receive the human condition in all its brokenness and frailty.

You can't help but laugh. You can't help but gasp. You are unnerved.

At the age of twelve, I was introduced to the Theatre of the Absurd at a summer arts camp high in the mountains of Southern California. Ionesco's *The Chairs*, which features a ninety-two-year-old man, was the first show I performed. I was shy eighty years, so right there, pretty absurd if you think about it. In subsequent summers, came *The Bald Soprano* and Albee's *The Sandbox*. This genre indelibly etched into my heart and mind a perspective on the world that has informed my life and my professional career as an artist on stage, in television and film. It cannot be by coincidence that I also met Saknussemm a couple of summers later at that same arts camp and we realized we had a shared experience of the 'odd.' This led to a life-long friendship that has included adventures into derelict America, *Twilight Zone* marathon viewings, and a keen, mutual appreciation of the bizarre.

When it comes to **odd**, Sak is the master. Whether it is a short story, novel, or play, he is able to find the 'disturbing' in the commonplace and conversely, the ordinary in the 'unusual.' I can only hope that you are as touched, disquieted, and enlightened by *The Humble Assessment* as I am.

***

In 1981, Phil Abrams began his professional acting career in San Francisco, starring in *Memory Hotel* at the renowned Magic Theatre. He continued performing at many local theatre companies before relocating to NYC. After a stint touring internationally with *The Reduced Shakespeare Company*, Phil relocated to Hollywood in the 90s. His film credits include *White Frog, The Island, Nancy Drew, Saving Sarah Cain* and close to one-hundred television shows with a variety of recurring roles and guest stars: *The Office, The Big Bang Theory, ER, Lost* and NBC's *Parenthood*, to name but a few.

The Humble Assessment

THE CHARACTERS

Mr. Humble: A disheveled and yet still somehow overly neat man in his mid 50s. Classic drab suit and tie.

Interviewer 1: Female, late 30s. Wears a formal skirt and expensive high heel shoes, but on top wears only a black lace bra.

Interviewer 2: A man of indeterminate age in a wheelchair.

Operations Manager: A man in a white tuxedo and a rubber gorilla mask.

Applicant #4: A man who appears wrapped in bandages like the Invisible Man.

THE SETTING

Nominally, an office in the Human Resources/Personnel division of a large anonymous company. But the stage is virtually bare, other than a long, unusually wide desk and some unexpected furnishings, which attract no special notice from the actors.

[*The stage is pitch dark. We hear the hints of ambient street noises and unidentified mechanical sounds...then a disembodied, machinelike voice over the PA system.*]

VOICE
I have lived and died long enough to see the towers of shimmering glass fleshed over their skeletons of Chinese steel rise above the hopes and the hopeless that hide in the crevices below...creating a necropolis of shadows, where there is neither light nor darkness, but rather a perpetual state of sustained dwindling...grief verging on rage...the gluttony of starvation...empty cocktail laughter and menus better read than eaten from.

Beneath the shining pillars of uncertainty, the streets are filled with forms that resemble people, better photographed than met.

And I am one of them, a denizen and not a citizen, of a wilderness of billboards...an oasis that erases...a vast bazaar that retails ever more ingenious forms of crisis to bewitch us into believing that the marionette machine still works.

But of course it works. Of course. For if it were ever to stop... even for a moment...

[*The voice distorts into a mess of static and we hear fragments of mangled news reports:*]

The stock market was down again today...
The alleged shooter will make his first court appearance...
Protesters have taken to the streets of...
More violence rips the capital in...

[*The voices and static end with a sharp mechanical clunk.*]

ACT I

INTERVIEWER 1 *sits at a three-quarter angle with her back to us. We never see the person's face.* The INTERVIEWER'S *chair is noticeably taller than the chair* HUMBLE *will occupy, so that the* INTERVIEWER *is always looking down, and* HUMBLE *always looking up, when seated.*

The suggestion of the office is almost entirely in shadow, but lights beat down on the surface of the desk, which is polished to a mirror-like finish.

On the desk is what looks like an empty goldfish bowl. The INTERVIEWER *is eating a piece of cake on a paper plate when* HUMBLE *arrives. The* INTERVIEWER *also has before her a big ledger pad and a pen in a holder. With each entry made in the ledger during the interview, the pen is returned to the holder, so that there is an overtly ceremonial intensity to each notation.*

On the floor beside the desk is an opened enormous white umbrella.

[HUMBLE *wanders in vaguely out of the dark, clutching a bunch of flowers, which he absently drops on the floor the moment he passes out of the shadows into the light. The light seems especially harsh on him when he finally sits down.*]

INTERVIEWER 1
[*Looks up, mouth full of cake.*] What's your view on disabled parking for obese people?

HUMBLE
Excuse me?

INTERVIEWER 1
[*Swallows, wipes mouth.*] Come in, Mr. Crumble.

HUMBLE
Humble.

INTERVIEWER 1
You're humble? Well, don't be shy too. Take a seat.

HUMBLE
I'm *a* Humble. [*He sits down rather gingerly, obviously vexed by the height of the chair.*]

INTERVIEWER 1
A humble what?

HUMBLE
That's my name. Richard Humble. Didn't you—

INTERVIEWER 1
I'm sorry about that.

HUMBLE
[*Smiles.*] Are you…making fun?

INTERVIEWER 1
Why? I'm sure plenty of others have done that.

HUMBLE
[*Now a bit miffed.*] I haven't gotten *your* name...the girl on the desk—

INTERVIEWER 1
No, you got a rather silly name. But I'll just call you 16.

HUMBLE
16? You've done 15 interviews for this position?

INTERVIEWER 1
Why would you think that?

HUMBLE
Because you just said 16...

INTERVIEWER 1
That's only because it's an easy number for me to remember. Are you trying to work out the odds—what your chances are?

HUMBLE
Well, I'd like...

INTERVIEWER 1
Given your age—and from what I know of actuarial tables—I'm not sure you'd like to know the odds of you even still being alive.

HUMBLE
Now wait a...

INTERVIEWER 1
Do you know how many men your age have had fatal strokes? I had a younger man than you keel over right in this very office. Same chair you're sitting in. You should've heard the sound when his head hit the desk. Actually, I think a stroke is the wrong way to put it. It was more like a massive cerebral hemorrhage. Doesn't something like one in three men your age suffer from impotence?

HUMBLE
W-what?

INTERVIEWER 1
I'm sorry, erectile dysfunction. I can see why the term impotence would worry you. Dysfunctional sounds better than impotent, doesn't it?

HUMBLE
What are you talking about?

INTERVIEWER 1
Are you being treated? I've heard there are side effects.

HUMBLE
Listen, I'm here to apply...I thought this was an interview for—

INTERVIEWER 1
My job? Is that what you'd like? You'd like to run the interview? Sit on my side of the desk...watching as all the miserable, washed up suits with their pink slip faces wander in, begging not to be thrown on the scrap heap?

HUMBLE
Look, I don't know what the story is here, but I just came for an interview. I had an appointment. The financial controller position.

INTERVIEWER 1
Is control an issue for you?

HUMBLE
Pardon?

INTERVIEWER 1
Well, you seem to want to take control of this interview. Why is that, 16?

HUMBLE
I don't want to take control of anything. I just—

INTERVIEWER 1
So, you don't want to help keep the company's financials in line and drive us toward greater profitability and sustained growth?

HUMBLE
[*Voice rising.*] I didn't say that, I said—

INTERVIEWER 1
How about self control?

HUMBLE
Is this a joke?

INTERVIEWER 1
Do you know any good jokes?

HUMBLE
Are you kidding?

INTERVIEWER 1
Is that your idea of a joke?

HUMBLE
What do you mean?

INTERVIEWER 1
I asked if you knew any good jokes. A test of your flexibility—quickness of mind. Your ability to relate and connect. Communication, lateral thinking. Financial controllers don't just manage numbers, they have to integrate with the whole of the business. They have to understand people as well as figures. Is that why you lost your last job?

HUMBLE
I didn't lose my last job. I resigned. Didn't you read my letter of application?

INTERVIEWER 1
Well that *is* something of a joke. I read your whole file. Says you enjoy cigars and 16-year-old bourbon.

[THE HUMBLE ASSESSMENT]

HUMBLE
What's...wrong with that?

INTERVIEWER 1
When's the last time you had any 16-year-old bourbon?

HUMBLE
Listen...I...

INTERVIEWER 1
And your favorite song is "Sixteen Tons" by Tennessee Ernie Ford.

HUMBLE
I didn't say anything like that.

INTERVIEWER 1
You might as well have. In response to our personal interest questionnaire, you've listed Glenn Ford as your favorite movie actor. Glenn Ford!

HUMBLE
So?

INTERVIEWER 1
Do you know that 95% of the people working for this company are too young to even know who Glenn Ford was? You go on to cite *Fate is the Hunter* as your favorite film. I had to Google on that. Suzanne Pleshette was in it too. What a saucy little strumpet she was in her day. She the kind who does it for you?

HUMBLE
I don't like your tone.

INTERVIEWER 1
And there the list ends. Have you ever heard the expression, "As boring as bat shit?"

HUMBLE
That's very rude. I—

INTERVIEWER 1
No hobbies listed!

HUMBLE
Well...

INTERVIEWER 1
You don't collect stamps. Don't play racquetball.

HUMBLE
I...

INTERVIEWER 1
No golf. Or fly-fishing. You don't build purple martin feeders or coach Little League.

HUMBLE
I used to coach Little League.

INTERVIEWER 1
You really think that's a skill base we should take into account?

HUMBLE
Look...don't you want to know what software packages I'm familiar with? The scale of businesses I've worked with?

INTERVIEWER 1
Software packages. Yes...spreadsheets and debit columns. Very important. May I offer you some sponge cake? Angel food sponge cake.

HUMBLE
[*Fuming.*] No...thank you.

INTERVIEWER 1
You know the secret of angel food sponge cake? It has to be moist. Moist and light. Lighter than air. Then you don't feel guilty eating it. Right?

[THE HUMBLE ASSESSMENT]

HUMBLE
I have over 25 years of experience…

INTERVIEWER 1
You look like you do.

HUMBLE
Is this some sort of new interview technique? Insult people—try to get them off balance?

INTERVIEWER 1
Do you feel off balance? Off kilter…out of whack?

HUMBLE
[*Slides awkwardly off the chair and has to right himself.*] No! I'm just…

INTERVIEWER 1
Just what? Eager to take someone else's job?

HUMBLE
No…I…

INTERVIEWER 1
Steal someone's livelihood right out from under them. Move a meal from one table to yours? All you can eat.

HUMBLE
I thought there was a vacancy.

INTERVIEWER 1
Vacancy?

HUMBLE
I thought the position had just opened.

INTERVIEWER 1
Vacancy? Vacancy is a not quite empty parking lot where a young girl was brutally raped. What would you know about vacancy—except for the vacancy inside yourself? I'd hate to be

behind you in a buffet line.

HUMBLE
Now wait a minute! I'm getting—I just meant I thought you had an opening.

INTERVIEWER 1
You're thinking about my openings?

HUMBLE
You know what I mean!

INTERVIEWER 1
This isn't a new position we recently created. How do you think it opened? Magically for you because you wished for it? I bet you haven't even given it a thought.

HUMBLE
Well, I just assumed…

INTERVIEWER 1
And made an ass of you and me.

HUMBLE
How did it open?

INTERVIEWER 1
Poor Mr. Cable.

HUMBLE
Who's Mr. Cable?

INTERVIEWER 1
John Cable. He was the guy who was in the job you're trying to wheedle your way into.

HUMBLE
I'm not trying to weasel my way into anything. I had an appointment.

[THE HUMBLE ASSESSMENT]

INTERVIEWER 1
I said wheedle. Poor John.

HUMBLE
What—happened to him?

INTERVIEWER 1
A good five years younger than you too.

HUMBLE
Did he—die?

INTERVIEWER 1
Collapsed in the men's room. In one of the stalls. Sat there on the crapper overnight. How undignified huh? Turning blue and stiff with your pants down at your knees.

HUMBLE
That's...terrible...I had no—

INTERVIEWER 1
Derek Whiteley had to kick down the stall door when he didn't answer. A good five years younger than you too.

HUMBLE
I...

INTERVIEWER 1
The toilet seat came with him when Derek lifted the body off. Isn't that awful?

HUMBLE
I'm sorry...to hear...

INTERVIEWER 1
You know what was even worse?

HUMBLE
I...

INTERVIEWER 1
This is *really* bad. But it's kind of funny too. [*She snorts.*] In a sick, tragic way.

HUMBLE
I had no...

INTERVIEWER 1
Poor old John...almost six years younger than you...he had this huge erection. Derek said it looked like he was choking the chihuahua when his heart exploded.

HUMBLE
[*Shivers.*] That's just...

INTERVIEWER 1
A simply giant hard-on—with the toilet seat stuck to his ass—his face all blue. Of course everyone knew he was hung like a donkey, because at the Christmas party last year he flopped it out for everyone to see. Just laid it right down on the table next to the pigs in a blanket. I swear, it was like two Coke cans with a lemon on top. Absolutely disgusting to think of him using that on his wife. It would be like giving birth every time.

HUMBLE
I don't want to hear any more...please...

INTERVIEWER 1
Of course, I don't think his wife saw much of it, because he mainly used it on his staff. Liked Hispanic women. Do you like Hispanic women?

HUMBLE
No!

INTERVIEWER 1
You have a problem with Hispanic people? Race issues?

HUMBLE
No!

[THE HUMBLE ASSESSMENT]

INTERVIEWER 1
We employ many Hispanic people, and racial harmony and respect is one of our key corporate values.

HUMBLE
I'm just—

INTERVIEWER 1
Back in the days when you could achieve a passable erection, would you have described yourself as a Shower or a Grower?

HUMBLE
Are you kidding—me?

INTERVIEWER 1
John Cable was both a Shower and a Grower. Do you know that once the toilet seat—and a fair bit of the skin of his ass was peeled away—they had to stick that big thing down with masking tape? Came up over his belly button.

HUMBLE
I...

INTERVIEWER 1
So, that's how the job you're hustling and groveling for "opened" up.

HUMBLE
I'm not groveling!

INTERVIEWER 1
Have you ever been convicted of a major felony?

HUMBLE
No. Of course not.

INTERVIEWER 1
Ever wished upon a falling star?

HUMBLE
What? I explained that I went out on my own, as a consultant—

INTERVIEWER 1
Yes, but you couldn't manage your own finances and now you've come crawling back to get a regular paycheck. Back to the teat for mother's milk.

HUMBLE
Look that's not—

INTERVIEWER 1
Do you know how many times I've heard that, 16? More than 16 times I can tell you.

HUMBLE
Please stop calling me that. My name is Humble.

INTERVIEWER 1
I think we've established that, 16, and I'll give you one out of ten on the joke test. But I've yet to see any actual humility. Which frankly surprises me. Yet here you sit, privately fawning and squirming, hankering for a lifeline that will help you meet your crushing mortgage payments each month.

HUMBLE
I've owned my house outright for over five years!

INTERVIEWER 1
I wager it's been refinanced and that you have difficulty maintaining an erection. I note that you're single. The three may be intimately related.

HUMBLE
[*Quietly.*] My wife died three years ago in a car accident.

INTERVIEWER 1
[*Utterly unmoved.*] So you *do* have difficulty maintaining an erection?

HUMBLE
What? Are you—

INTERVIEWER 1
Well, you're still single three years later. Connect the dots, 16. Three for three. Everything is related.

HUMBLE
Listen, if you're not going to ask me some relevant questions about my qualifications…

INTERVIEWER 1
What's not relevant about your psychological state, 16? Why should we hire a lonely, possibly impotent, embittered man?

HUMBLE
Embittered?

INTERVIEWER 1
Is that how you'd describe yourself, 16? Now we're getting somewhere.

HUMBLE
I'm not embittered.

INTERVIEWER 1
Well, that's to your credit, given the erection difficulties.

HUMBLE
[*Shouts.*] I don't have a problem with my erections! I'm seeing someone.

INTERVIEWER 1
A psychiatrist?

HUMBLE
A woman! I'm seeing a woman!

INTERVIEWER 1
Seeing? As in watching? Are you a peeping tom? A stalker?

HUMBLE
NO! I have a girlfriend, thank you. She's just...

INTERVIEWER 1
Just what?

HUMBLE
She's married. All right.

INTERVIEWER 1
So, you'd break up another man's home to fuel your ravenous middle-aged lust. Typical. See what I mean about the buffet line?

HUMBLE
This is what's insane!

INTERVIEWER 1
What's insane, 16? Your hope of ever getting employed again?

HUMBLE
No! This! This farce of an interview. It's a joke.

INTERVIEWER 1
You didn't do well on the joke test, 16. Are you pleading for another chance?

HUMBLE
I'm not pleading for anything!

INTERVIEWER 1
So you don't want the job?

HUMBLE
Look, are you on some kind of medication?

INTERVIEWER 1
Tell me what you know about medication, 16.

HUMBLE
I'm not on any medication.

INTERVIEWER 1
I doubt that seriously, 16. A man your age.

HUMBLE
I'm not under any obligation to tell you something like that. It's illegal to ask.

INTERVIEWER 1
[*Takes pen from the holder and writes in ledger.*] Difficult, uncommunicative…suspicious verging on paranoid…[*Replaces pen.*]

HUMBLE
I'm leaving.

INTERVIEWER 1
Like you did your last job. [*Takes pen from the holder and writes in ledger.*] No commitment, lack of focus. First man in the lifeboat. [*Replaces pen.*]

HUMBLE
[*Open-mouthed with disbelief.*] Are you completely crazy?

INTERVIEWER 1
What does crazy mean to you, 16?

HUMBLE
This!

INTERVIEWER 1
You think this company is crazy? You want to work for a company that's crazy? That doesn't seem very sensible, does it?

HUMBLE
No, it doesn't. I've changed my mind.

INTERVIEWER 1
So, I can scratch you off the list?

HUMBLE
Yes, you can. I wouldn't work for this stupid company if you paid me.

INTERVIEWER 1
Well, that was the general idea. We were actually thinking of paying you 15% more than what you indicated, with a bonus package for targets met.

HUMBLE
You...were? You mean...

INTERVIEWER 1
Yes. But I understand your point of view. Thank you for stopping by.

HUMBLE
That's it? [*Starts to rise.*]

INTERVIEWER 1
That's what?

HUMBLE
I don't get the job? [*Sits down again.*]

INTERVIEWER 1
You said you didn't want the job. [*Takes pen from the holder and writes in ledger.*] Wishy-washy, unable to make clear-cut decisions.

HUMBLE
I didn't know I had the job!

INTERVIEWER 1
[*Replaces pen.*] What did you hope to accomplish in this interview?

HUMBLE
I...uh...

INTERVIEWER 1
[*Takes pen from the holder and writes in ledger.*] Unable to form definite goals, easily distracted, combative.

HUMBLE
I'm not combative!

INTERVIEWER 1
Listen 16—

HUMBLE
Humble! My name is Humble!

INTERVIEWER 1
And I'm sorry about that, but I think we're done here. [*Replaces pen.*]

HUMBLE
But I had the job!

INTERVIEWER 1
You did once have a job, yes. I read that.

HUMBLE
No! This job.

INTERVIEWER 1
My job? You're back to wanting my job?

HUMBLE
I'm talking about the controller position.

INTERVIEWER 1
[*Takes pen from holder and writes in ledger.*] Continuously seeks a control position.

HUMBLE
I don't want control!

INTERVIEWER 1
Unable to take responsibility.

HUMBLE
I just want a job!

INTERVIEWER 1
I see. So you have been pleading and begging the whole time? [*Replaces pen.*]

HUMBLE
I…yeah…jeez, whatever you say.

INTERVIEWER 1
Well, then. What would you do to get this job? You've asked me to wipe you off the list, to take you out of the running—and now you want to be reinstated. Just like that. Snap! To be back in the competition. To have a chance. What would you do for me to give you that chance?

HUMBLE
What do you mean?

INTERVIEWER 1
[*Takes pen from holder and writes in ledger.*] Slow comprehension, overly cautious.

HUMBLE
What do you mean? I thought I had the job?

INTERVIEWER 1
You did once have a job, apparently. But what would you do for this one? [*Replaces pen.*]

HUMBLE
I don't understand.

INTERVIEWER 1
Do you have a hearing impairment, 16? You should've advised us in your letter of application.

HUMBLE
I don't have a hearing problem!

INTERVIEWER 1
What?

HUMBLE
I don't have a hearing problem!

INTERVIEWER 1
[*Takes pen from holder and writes in ledger.*] Severe mood swings. Anger management issues.

HUMBLE
I just don't understand is all! What do you mean, what would I do for the job?

INTERVIEWER 1
[*Replaces pen.*] Well, for instance...would you...stand on that chair and crow like a chicken?

HUMBLE
What?

INTERVIEWER 1
It's standard procedure for executive hiring in Japan.

HUMBLE
You want me to stand on this chair...and...

INTERVIEWER 1
Would you prefer to stand on the desk?

HUMBLE
You want me to crow...like a chicken?

INTERVIEWER 1
Are you questioning proven Japanese management methods?

HUMBLE
You seriously want me to stand on this chair and crow like a chicken?

INTERVIEWER 1
You can crow as seriously as you like. Or, you could be exuberant and proud. Pleased to be employed again. Safely reconnected

to a vitalizing income stream and validated as a virile man in society once more. No more depressive naps in the afternoon. No more nips at 11 AM. No more melancholy walks in the park, wondering where it all went wrong.

HUMBLE
[*Shrugs in disbelief.*] Where it all went wrong…

INTERVIEWER 1
Think of the relief in knowing.

HUMBLE
[*Leaning forward across the desk.*] Listen, I don't take naps. I don't drink before 5 PM ever and I don't take walks!

INTERVIEWER 1
How much do you drink after 5?

HUMBLE
What?

INTERVIEWER 1
You know you should walk for at least 20 minutes every day. That was the problem with the man who keeled over in that very chair. You should've heard the sound he made when his head hit the desk.

HUMBLE
You want me to crow like a chicken…

INTERVIEWER 1
Do you want to crow like a chicken?

HUMBLE
If that's what it will take, I'll do it. [*He slowly climbs on top of the chair and after a moment's hesitation gives a ludicrous but anemic crow.*]

INTERVIEWER 1
Is that the best you can do? Seriously?

[HUMBLE *crows again more forcefully, while flapping his arms.*]

INTERVIEWER 1
Bravo. And I especially applaud the self-styled choreography. But frankly, that still sounded more like a hen being molested by a rooster—which brings us back to the erectile issue.

HUMBLE
I DON'T have a problem with my erections!

INTERVIEWER 1
[*Cheering.*] That's the spirit! That's the therapy of positive thinking! Conquer your weaknesses.

HUMBLE
I don't have a problem getting it up, all right?

INTERVIEWER 1
So you keep saying.

HUMBLE
You want me to crow louder? Is that it?

INTERVIEWER 1
Do you want to crow louder?

HUMBLE
[*He lets loose with a very loud screeching crow.*] EEEEE—AHHH—EEEYYYY!

INTERVIEWER 1
[*Pause.*] My word. Now that *was* something. You really made a cock of yourself that time, Dick.

HUMBLE
Richard.

INTERVIEWER 1
16.

HUMBLE
Humble! My name is Humble! [*Tries to step off the chair and falls.*]

INTERVIEWER 1
[*Takes pen from holder and writes in ledger.*] Self-esteem issues, takes himself very seriously.

HUMBLE
Goddamn it! [*Regains his chair.*]

INTERVIEWER 1
Manic tendencies.

[HUMBLE *slams his hand down on the desk.*]

INTERVIEWER 1
There! That's what the man who had the brain hemorrhage sounded like when his head hit the desk! That's almost *exactly* what it sounded like. Do you know they later found out he was bleeding from one ear. Imagine it. Not a nosebleed, an earbleed. [*Replaces pen.*]

HUMBLE
I can imagine.

INTERVIEWER 1
That was a sterling effort, it really was. But I think you should feel grateful.

HUMBLE
Yeah? Why?

INTERVIEWER 1
[*Pause.*] Do you see that goldfish bowl there?

HUMBLE
Yeah. I see it.

INTERVIEWER 1
You think it's empty, right?

HUMBLE
I can *see* that it's empty.

INTERVIEWER 1
Well, you know what we've done in the past with these hiring consultations?

HUMBLE
I shudder to think.

INTERVIEWER 1
We've had that bowl filled with live crickets. Quite a lot of them. Shiny black crickets. Very active. Had to have a big cork stopper with breathing holes punched through. It's not really a goldfish bowl. It was originally a gumball jar. We tried dung beetles, but the crickets were more interesting. Do you know why we had the crickets?

HUMBLE
I can't even begin...

INTERVIEWER 1
Because we're a gung-ho company with a sense of play and fun, 16. We're sponsors! We sponsor a tarantula. How many companies do you know who can say that?

HUMBLE
I can't think of a single—

INTERVIEWER 1
The creature came into the country in a shipment of imported furniture. You know...jungle bric-a-brac made in a monsoon sweatshop in some malaria republic where sniveling locals work for peanuts and are damn glad of the chance. It was seized by customs and taken on by the museum. It's now in quarantine, more or less permanently. It likes crickets. The livelier the better. The museum had the idea of putting a web cam in its enclosure. Do you want to see it? We could check on what it's up to right now.

HUMBLE
You want me to watch a tarantula?

[*Behind* HUMBLE, *so that he doesn't notice, but the audience certainly does, a screen illuminates and we see projected a tarantula being fed crickets by hand. It's only a short video made by a museum, but projected onto the screen it takes on giant, frightening and also curiously hypnotic proportions.*]

INTERVIEWER 1
It's a rather poignant story of dignity in captivity, which I think you should appreciate.

HUMBLE
I don't want to watch a big hairy spider. I'm applying for—

INTERVIEWER 1
Aren't you at least curious about why we filled the bowl with crickets?

HUMBLE
Tell me.

INTERVIEWER 1
We sponsor the tarantula, so, that gave us a connection with a company that raises the crickets. That's where I got them.

HUMBLE
Yeah…

INTERVIEWER 1
And sometimes we videotape these employment sessions.

HUMBLE
What?

INTERVIEWER 1
I got the idea from watching the tarantula. The staff here really enjoy going online at feeding time and seeing how the spider's doing. It's a female and we call her Ernestine. It brings people

together on Friday afternoons. Better than endless drinks or some inane barbecue, yes? We now sponsor another Cobalt Blue tarantula—and a hognose snake too.

HUMBLE
You videotape these private interview sessions? Is that what you just said?

INTERVIEWER 1
I thought it would be of benefit to staff to provide a sort of spider cam insight into just what people are willing to do to get employed here.

HUMBLE
Do you know that's totally against the law…not to mention…

INTERVIEWER 1
I got prospective employees—the hopefuls just like yourself—to try their hand at eating live crickets.

[*The image of the tarantula behind* HUMBLE *fades, and we see a man who looks very much like him, only wearing a different suit, thrusting his hand into the fishbowl, which appears to be filled with what might be crickets. Ravenously, shamelessly, the man stuffs his mouth with the contents.*]

HUMBLE
That's the most twisted thing I've ever heard.

INTERVIEWER 1
Really? You've been out of the corporate hiring loop for quite some time. You'd be surprised at the alacrity of some of our contestants. I love that word, "alacrity." Says it all.

HUMBLE
You could be sued for that.

INTERVIEWER 1
One man in similar dire straits to you holds the record. He gobbled up every last cricket in 16 seconds. 16 seconds flat. Some

of the crickets got away—he had to scurry around on the floor to catch them. It was impressive.

HUMBLE
Totally…

INTERVIEWER 1
Pathetic—but impressive. I think the staff enjoyed it. Something of a morale boost to witness the frenzy. And confirmation of course…just how lucky they are to be employed. You've probably applied for at least 16 jobs, haven't you?

HUMBLE
You…are…

INTERVIEWER 1
I'm certain they'll enjoy your chicken squawk. Let's move on shall we? [*The screen behind goes dark.*] Now I don't want you under any circumstances to think of a hippopotamus. [*A hippo illuminates the screen.*] Or, I might add…a voluptuous naked woman… oozing sexual appeal…with full, firm breasts and hair you can almost smell. All right? [*The hippo dissolves into a naked woman, and then the actress Suzanne Pleshette appears.*] Don't think of Suzanne Pleshette either.

HUMBLE
Very funny. [*The image and the screen fade into darkness.*]

INTERVIEWER 1
16, I know you think my methods are unorthodox.

HUMBLE
Try certifiable.

INTERVIEWER 1
One man's meat. At least I get results. Do you know I've reduced restroom time for our call center staff by 43%? A numbers man should welcome that. 43 is a significant number. A 43-year-old woman would be a much younger woman for you, wouldn't it?

HUMBLE
You enjoy baiting people don't you?

INTERVIEWER 1
[*Oblivious.*] And I've established a very effective oversee system so that non-management staff are continuously monitored to maintain maximum effectiveness and esprit de corps.

HUMBLE
[*Still more disbelief.*] You *spy* on your staff?

INTERVIEWER 1
No more than we keep tabs on the tarantula. We just want to know how many crickets our people are catching—so to speak. As I told you, you've been out of the game a long time. Today it's all about productivity and value. It's no longer a pat on the back just for showing up.

HUMBLE
You can't spy on people. Your own employees.

INTERVIEWER 1
Well, it's a lot easier than spying on other companies' employees. But I think we're having a semantic tug of war. What I'm talking about is discreet observation and rigorous protection of benchmarks. There's absolutely no reason in the world why Linda Jacobi in Logistics should have more time to sit on the toilet than Marilyn Thoroughgood in Corporate Affairs.

HUMBLE
Maybe she needs more time.

INTERVIEWER 1
Why? Because of diet, stress, tensions at home…drug use, some sort of gynecological malfunction? I think the company has every right to know about such things, because they impact her job performance and her ability to catch crickets. If we'd had as many cameras in operation as I've requested, John Cable wouldn't have sat there in rigor mortis overnight.

HUMBLE
You should be reported.

INTERVIEWER 1
That's life in the big city.

HUMBLE
You should be taken to court.

INTERVIEWER 1
But you still want the job.

HUMBLE
The media will hear about this.

INTERVIEWER 1
Get down off your high horse.

[HUMBLE *looks up feebly.*]

INTERVIEWER 1
You still want the job.

HUMBLE
You don't actually have cameras in the restrooms? Do you?

INTERVIEWER 1
Give me your hand.

HUMBLE
No.

INTERVIEWER 1
Give me your hand.

HUMBLE
[*Almost childishly this time.*] No. [*From an initial retraction, he at last offers up his hand, as if it's not really part of his body.*]

[THE HUMBLE ASSESSMENT]

INTERVIEWER 1
Now, it's time to get down to brass tacks. And I just happen to have one right here. [*The* INTERVIEWER *produces what we take to be a pin and jabs one of* HUMBLE'S *fingers.*]

HUMBLE
OW!

INTERVIEWER 1
Oh, don't be such a big baby. Quick, we need to get it fresh. [*The* INTERVIEWER *produces a Kleenex and dabs the finger, smearing the blood. Then holds up the Kleenex.*] There! What do you see?

HUMBLE
My blood. And a…lunatic.

INTERVIEWER 1
Well, we hope it's your blood. But what do you see in it—the picture that it forms? Haven't you ever heard of a Rorschach test?

HUMBLE
I'm still bleeding.

INTERVIEWER 1
I don't doubt that on any level. But what do you see? This is important for your psychological profile.

HUMBLE
A butterfly.

INTERVIEWER 1
Really?

HUMBLE
A butterfly of my blood.

INTERVIEWER 1
How disappointingly unoriginal.

HUMBLE
A sheep's head then.

INTERVIEWER 1
You know what that indicates?

HUMBLE
All right, I see an ogre eating a flower. Or just a heart. Broken down the middle.

INTERVIEWER 1
Turn it around…and it looks rather like a lipstick stain on a napkin…or a shirt collar. Doesn't it?

HUMBLE
If you say so.

INTERVIEWER 1
May I see your driver's license?

HUMBLE
I don't have it with me.

INTERVIEWER 1
Don't have it with you—or don't have one?

HUMBLE
I don't have it with me.

INTERVIEWER 1
Why's that?

HUMBLE
I just forgot. Then when I remembered, it was too late to go back.

INTERVIEWER 1
You didn't list a driver's license number in your application. Are you sure you have one?

HUMBLE
Yes, I'm sure.

INTERVIEWER 1
But you don't remember the number?

HUMBLE
Who remembers their license number?

INTERVIEWER 1
What's your license *plate* number?

HUMBLE
I don't currently own a vehicle.

INTERVIEWER 1
I noticed you didn't include one in your salary package expectations. Worried about your carbon footprint? Or did you lose your license? Drunk driving? Some regrettable accident?

HUMBLE
[*Pause.*] I just forgot to bring my license.

INTERVIEWER 1
How did you get to this interview? Cab? Public transport?

HUMBLE
I took the train.

INTERVIEWER 1
And maybe a bus too. Why would you think of going back for your driver's license, if you weren't going to be driving?

HUMBLE
Well, it's always good to be able to identify yourself.

INTERVIEWER 1
To know who you are?

HUMBLE
To be able to validate who you are.

INTERVIEWER 1
And you forgot your validation. I notice you're not wearing a watch either.

HUMBLE
It's getting repaired. I left with plenty of time, and there are lots of clocks around in the city.

INTERVIEWER 1
I'm sure at your stage that's the way it seems everywhere.

[*A mechanized offstage voice announces:* **THE NEXT PHASE OF THE EVALUATION IS ABOUT TO COMMENCE.** *A red light like an ambulance's comes on and begins spinning.*]

INTERVIEWER 1
That's my cue. The fur's going to really fly now. Just kidding. Good luck.

HUMBLE
What...?

INTERVIEWER 1
[*She slips out of her chair and saunters over to him, still with her back to us.*] Do you like my perfume? I like that aftershave you're wearing. Has the smell of desperation. [*Then she leans into him, pushing her breasts into his face.*] Go get 'em big boy.

[*She gives a malicious giggle and goes over to pick up the white umbrella. She twirls it and then clocks off on her high heels into the shadows. The stage goes dark and we hear the Tom Jones version of "Sixteen Tons."*]

ACT II

HUMBLE *sits just as* INTERVIEWER 1 *left him, only he is now wearing handcuffs, which he seems to take no notice of.*

From out of the shadows in the corner of the implied room staggers the OPERATIONS MANAGER *in white tuxedo and gorilla mask. He seems fixated on a Rubik's Cube type of mechanical puzzle.*

[*The lights come up full and hot.*]

OM
Say, do you know how to work these things? I've been at this damn gimmick for as long as I can remember.

HUMBLE
Where did you come from?

OM
What?

HUMBLE
Have you been here the whole time?

OM
What whole time?

HUMBLE
My interview.

OM
You've had an interview?

HUMBLE
Were you in here listening?

OM
Did she make you eat any crickets?

HUMBLE
Were you spying on my interview?

OM
I liked your chicken crow in the end.

HUMBLE
So, you *were* spying.

OM
Took you a while to get warmed up. But you pulled it off.

HUMBLE
Why were you spying on my interview? What gives you the right?

OM
Have you ever solved one of these puzzle things? Blasted waste of time if you ask me.

HUMBLE
Are you here for an interview?

OM
What?

HUMBLE
Are you here for an interview?

OM
You're conducting interviews?

HUMBLE
No! You just heard me *being* interviewed—because you were spying.

OM
I liked your chicken crow in the end.

HUMBLE
Who are you? Why are you here?

OM
Took you a while to get warmed up. But you pulled it off.

HUMBLE
Are you here for an interview?

OM
So you *are* conducting interviews.

HUMBLE
I'm NOT conducting interviews!

OM
Then why do you keep asking me if I'm here for an interview?

HUMBLE
I'm trying to work out what you're doing in this room…hiding and spying on my interview session!

OM
Can't you see? I'm trying to work out this damn puzzle. What position are you applying for?

HUMBLE
That's none of your business.

OM
How can you be so sure?

HUMBLE
Why are you here?

OM
Maybe because it's my business.

HUMBLE
So, you're not applying for the financial controller's position?

OM
Are you applying for the financial controller's position?

HUMBLE
You heard all of that—because you were spying!

OM
I wasn't really spying. I was trying to work out this stupid cube.

HUMBLE
But why were you hiding in here—during my interview? Are you

applying for another position?

OM
Oh, God no.

HUMBLE
Is this another part of the interview process?

OM
You're asking me?

HUMBLE
Why don't you answer?

OM
Why do you keep asking me questions and then insisting you're not conducting an interview?

HUMBLE
What position are you applying for?

OM
You see?

HUMBLE
No, I don't. I want to know what job you're applying for.

OM
None.

HUMBLE
So, you're one of the interviewers?

OM
Well, I suppose I could be. But I'm not. I'm the Operations Manager.

HUMBLE
You can't be.

OM
What have you heard? Are they sharpening the knives?

HUMBLE
What knives?

OM
You're interviewing again.

HUMBLE
I'm just saying it's unlikely that you're the Operations Manager.

OM
Do you know something I don't?

HUMBLE
Because…well, why are you wearing that ridiculous mask?

OM
Didn't you get the memo?

HUMBLE
What memo? Of course I didn't get any memo. I don't work here yet. I've just come for an interview.

OM
For the financial controller's position. I liked your chicken crow in the end. Took you a while to get warmed up. But you pulled it off.

HUMBLE
Why the mask?

OM
It's Funny Friday. We're all supposed to inject some zaniness into the work place.

HUMBLE
It's not Friday! It's Monday!

OM
It is? Are you sure?

HUMBLE
My interview was scheduled for Monday.

OM
For the financial controller's position. I liked your chicken crow in the end. Took you a while to get warmed up. But you pulled it off.

HUMBLE
Today is Monday.

OM
So, it's not Friday.

HUMBLE
It can't be Friday if it's Monday!

OM
And you didn't get the memo.

HUMBLE
It's Monday!

OM
I must've been fiddling with this cube for longer than I thought.

HUMBLE
And that still doesn't explain why you were in here spying on me and the interview session.

OM
Oh, that's easy.

HUMBLE
Yes?

OM
What?

HUMBLE
What's the explanation?

OM
They're doing some work in my office. Secretly, I think they're installing a video camera to keep an eye on me, but the official reason is that they're doing some maintenance on the air conditioning system. All I know is that there's a lot of dust.

HUMBLE
What does that have to do with the price of fish in England?

OM
I'm not sure I follow you.

HUMBLE
It's an expression! What does dust in your office have to do with you being here…spying on me?

OM
I can't very well be in my office if there's dust everywhere, can I?

HUMBLE
So you hid in here?

OM
I wasn't hiding. Well, I didn't start out hiding. I went for a walk—and I was so caught up with this dumb cube, I didn't notice where I'd gotten to. Then you came in and I didn't want to interrupt. I liked your chicken crow in the end. Took you a while to get warmed up. But you pulled it off.

HUMBLE
I wish you'd stop reminding me of that. It's humiliating enough having done it at all.

OM
That HR gal's a hot number. I bet you were thinking of sticking it to her.

HUMBLE
I was not!

OM
So, what she was saying about the erection problems was right?

HUMBLE
NO! And I thought you were playing with your cube.

OM
I was mostly. But I heard your chicken crow. Probably everybody on this floor did. Took you a while to get in the groove. But you nailed it finally.

HUMBLE
Stop it.

OM
Too bad that's not part of the job description. If it came down to imitating a chicken, you'd ace it.

HUMBLE
Shut up!

OM
That's no way to talk to the Operations Manager. I can't believe it's not Friday.

HUMBLE
It's not even Thursday!

OM
I thought you said it was Monday. Of course it can't be Thursday. How would that work?

HUMBLE
[*Makes a move to pull off the gorilla mask.*] I want to see what you look like without that cheesy mask on.

OM
Now, now. Remember, I'm the Operations Manager. And you have to get ready for the next phase in the interview process.

HUMBLE
So, this wasn't it.

OM
Of course not.

HUMBLE
How can I be sure?

OM
Well, it's like you telling me this is Monday.

HUMBLE
It is Monday!

OM
You think it's Monday because your interview was scheduled for then.

HUMBLE
No, damn it! It IS Monday!

OM
That still doesn't mean this is part of the interview. Does it? Just because this is Monday doesn't make me one of the interviewers. Right?

HUMBLE
N-no.

OM
Although I think it's Friday.

[THE HUMBLE ASSESSMENT]

HUMBLE
IT'S MONDAY!

OM
How do you explain my Funny Friday attire?

HUMBLE
Because you're completely cracked! Or a nitwit.

OM
How can that be, if I'm the Operations Manager. It's not likely, is it? Think of the responsibilities. Do you know how big this company is?

[*The* OPERATIONS MANAGER *heads in the direction of what we take to be the door to the room, even though this is never clearly visualized.*]

OM
If I were you I'd start worrying about the next phase in the assessment. You'll have to do a lot more than screech like a chicken.

[*He does an imitation of* HUMBLE'S *crow and buckles over with laughter.*]

You did really well with that part in the end. If you manage to get hired, people will call you Chicken Man—or maybe Rooster, if you're lucky.

HUMBLE
Go to hell.

OM
Before the Cricket Man jumped off the executive parking lot roof, that's what everyone called him. The Cricket Man. Because he was the one to eat the most crickets ever. I couldn't tell you what his real name was. He was just the Cricket Man. You'll be the Chicken Man. That is, if you get the job—which isn't very likely.

49

HUMBLE
Why not? I'm perfectly well qualified.

OM
And you give good chicken. You're Funny Friday all by yourself.

HUMBLE
It's Monday, you idiot!

[*The* OPERATIONS MANAGER *disappears into the shadows, as if he has left the room, still chuckling.* HUMBLE *is left alone, and still seems not to notice that he's wearing handcuffs. He waits for an uncomfortable amount of time, as a strange noise begins to insinuate itself. It sounds like someone both bumping into and scratching upon a door. At last a figure appears, inching forward, wrapped in tattered and unraveling gauze bandages from head to foot, looking something like a mummy.*]

#4
Ugh.

HUMBLE
[*Starts with surprise.*] Who are you?

#4
[*Feeling his way forward, as though completely blind behind the bandages.*] I'm here for an interview. Another assessment.

HUMBLE
Are you an interviewer?

#4
I'm 4.

HUMBLE
You're an applicant.

#4
I'm undergoing another assessment. I'm 4.

HUMBLE
What happened to you? Are you hurt?

#4
I'm undergoing another assessment. I'm 4.

HUMBLE
Did they do this to you?

#4
I'm undergoing another assessment. I'm 4.

HUMBLE
Stop saying that and answer my question.

#4
Is this the next part of the interview?

HUMBLE
You can't be sure. Answer my question.

#4
I feel like I've been skinned alive.

HUMBLE
Who did this to you?

#4
I think I *have* been skinned alive.

HUMBLE
Don't be absurd. They wouldn't go that far.

#4
Who?

HUMBLE
The interviewers. This whole thing is mad—but they wouldn't dare physically hurt you. They might try to push you over some personal precipice…but they're not torturers.

#4
Precipice. [*He pauses a moment...and then lets out a hideous high-pitched cackle.*]

HUMBLE
Have you been burned?

#4
I'm 4.

HUMBLE
Tell me what happened?

#4
I'm 4.

HUMBLE
Stop that and tell me what happened.

#4
Interview.

HUMBLE
Which position are you applying for?

#4
Position?

HUMBLE
Job. Which job are you going for?

#4
Are you the next interviewer?

HUMBLE
I'm...an applicant. I'm Humble.

#4
I'm 4.

HUMBLE
No, I mean that's my name. Humble. Richard Humble. What's your name? [*No reply seems to be forthcoming.*] Your name. What's your name?

[#4 *stands motionless, not responding.*]

HUMBLE
What's that sound?

[#4 *stands motionless, not responding.*]

HUMBLE
Can you hear me? Are you all right? 4?

[#4 *remains motionless, not responding.*]

HUMBLE
Listen…what's that noise. Can you hear it? 4? It seems to be coming…from you…from inside the bandages…

[HUMBLE *goes to have a closer inspection of the bandaged man who has stopped dead still…when he suddenly ducks his head as if an angry insect had just buzzed at him. He takes a step nearer and peeks into a rent in the gauze wrappings…and then lets out a gurgle of terrified revulsion.*]

HUMBLE
My…God…you're…they're….

#4
I'm…4.

HUMBLE
You're filled…with…you're crawling…they're…

#4
I'm…4.

HUMBLE
You have to get out of here!

#4
I'm undergoing another assessment. I'm 4.

HUMBLE
You have to get out of here right now!

#4
I'm undergoing another assessment. I'm 4.

HUMBLE
The bandages…bees…hornets…

#4
I'm 4.

HUMBLE
You have to go right now! Before they…

#4
Are you an interviewer?

HUMBLE
…go wild. They'll swarm…attack!

#4
I'm an applicant.

HUMBLE
You're like a giant wasp's nest.

#4
I'm 4.

HUMBLE
They've turned you into a wasp's nest!

#4
I'm an applicant.

[HUMBLE *ducks and weaves as if more wasps have escaped the bandages. We hear the irritated buzzing sound more loudly.*]

HUMBLE
I'm sorry...but you're going to have to leave.

[*#4 seems to tremble all over.*]

HUMBLE
Get out! Go!

[*We hear the buzzing getting louder.*]

HUMBLE
Go! Get away! Out of the room! I'm allergic to bee stings. I could die.

#4
Is my interview over?

HUMBLE
Yes! I'm sorry. Leave now.

[*#4 begins to shake all over as if on the verge of an intense spasm or seizure.*]

HUMBLE
Go! Leave now!

[*#4's shaking becomes insane, the bandages tearing and flapping... and then with a banshee-like wail, he races stage left into the shadows and we hear the sound of broken glass, leaving us wondering if he's leapt out a window or crashed through a door...*

HUMBLE *gazes after him in disbelief—and relief.*]

HUMBLE
[*Under his breath.*] A beehive…wasp's nest…

[*He jerks his head as though one of the wasps is still in the room. He picks up the big ledger book and swats at it viciously. At last, he seems to have knocked it out of the air. He squashes it with one of his feet, grinding the shoe in with disturbing relish.*]

ACT III

INTERVIEWER 2 *sits in a wheelchair with his back to us.* HUMBLE *is no longer wearing handcuffs, but wavers on a kind of dangling seat, which suggests both a kids' swing set and a canary perch.*

Behind him are arranged three tall ladders, which cast ominous skeletal shadows.

With the slightly different lighting arrangement, we now see a pattern of hopscotch squares laid out on the floor.

On the desk is the empty goldfish bowl from before…along with the big ledger pad and the pen in its holder. But there has been added a very large, ornate hourglass and what appears to be a sinister looking welder's helmet, along with an immensely oversized Erlenmeyer flask, big enough to be a flower vase.

On the floor beside INTERVIEWER 2'S *wheelchair is a shiny black top hat.*

INTERVIEWER 2
Why do you suppose Sally sells seashells by the seashore?

HUMBLE
What?

INTERVIEWER 2
Well, isn't that like selling oil to the Arabs? Ice to the Eskimos? Wouldn't it make more sense to sell them in the city—or some place *away* from the seashore?

HUMBLE
What's this about now?

INTERVIEWER 2
It's a basic marketing question, Mr. Bumble.

HUMBLE
Humble.

INTERVIEWER 2
Bumble, rumble, tumble, mumble, stumble, fumble…I don't think you're getting my drift. This company has more than a little to do with marketing questions. Competitive advantages. Unique selling propositions. Supply channels, distribution networks, meeting customer needs.

HUMBLE
It doesn't mean anything.

INTERVIEWER 2
Meeting customer needs?

HUMBLE
Sally and the seashells. It's just a tongue tangler. A gimmick. Like—saying "toy boat" fast—or—

INTERVIEWER 2
Irish wrist watch? Round the rugged rock the ragged rascal ran… how much wood could a woodchuck chuck—that sort of thing?

HUMBLE
Yes.

INTERVIEWER 2
Um, perhaps. But it's funny...the things you can say fast...without thinking. And the things you have to think about. Raises some interesting questions about honesty, don't you agree?

HUMBLE
How do you mean?

INTERVIEWER 2
Well, on the one hand, honesty would appear to be what you can say without having to consider and plan. On the other hand, thinking suggests care and involvement with a particular question—or an individual. Not just a glib, automatic, mindless response—but an honest, intelligent assessment. Isn't that what we're all hoping for? An honest, thoughtful assessment? Isn't that what you want?

HUMBLE
Y-yes.

INTERVIEWER 2
I understand that you took the train in today. You're committed to conserving our petroleum resources. Do you take the train regularly?

HUMBLE
A bit.

INTERVIEWER 2
Do you recall the fairly large downtown train wreck we had three years ago?

HUMBLE
Of course.

INTERVIEWER 2
Are you aware that when all the debris was cleared away, all the

bodies tallied and the survivors looked after, there were ten people unaccounted for? You know what happened to those ten people?

HUMBLE
The Bermuda Triangle?

INTERVIEWER 2
Not far wrong in one sense. Ten people unknown to each other all decided that the train wreck and the resulting confusion gave them an opportunity to step out of their old lives and to disappear. Don't you find that remarkable?

HUMBLE
Well…

INTERVIEWER 2
Ten people mind you, not one or two. Ten strangers all got the same idea at the same time. And what a peculiar idea…to simply vaporize into the chaos…leave everything behind and begin again.

HUMBLE
Maybe they were just…

INTERVIEWER 2
What? In trouble? Bored? Leaving your old life behind isn't something you do lightly, is it? You have to wonder, were they planning to make a break and just waiting for the right opportunity. Did they have new lives—or double lives—already in place? Or was it some spur of the moment thing?

HUMBLE
Why are you telling me all this?

INTERVIEWER 2
I'm interested in what your thoughts are on the matter. The company is interested. You seem to think gaining employment here is merely a matter of qualifications and experience, which are a dime a dozen—things you've listed on a piece of paper. That's all very old school. Not to mention the fact that things that should

be on that piece of paper can be expunged or conveniently left off. Progressive enterprises today are concerned about the actual quality of thinking of their people. So, what's your theory?

HUMBLE
I really don't know. I doubt ten people who don't know each other would all have the same reason.

INTERVIEWER 2
Correct. Or so it would seem. Since the accident, what's come to light is the following. One man had been drinking heavily and seems to have just wandered off in a daze. He was found in a men's shelter two months later, suffering from short-term memory loss. Two others, a man and a woman, no connection, were months later tracked down by private investigators hired by family or friends. They could offer no concrete reason for their actions. They simply wanted to leave their old selves behind. Had they premeditated the act and made arrangements, they might've pulled it off. Two others, both male, were only recently apprehended by criminal authorities. It's clear they both had good reason to want to get away and were on the verge of doing so, whether the train had smashed or not. The remaining five are mysteriously still at large—and appear to have disappeared as completely as anyone can. [*Pause.*] Tell me, if you were going to escape your life, how would you do it? Where would you go?

HUMBLE
I haven't given that...much consideration. Who says I want to escape my life?

INTERVIEWER 2
Everyone wants to escape from something. [*Pats the arms of the wheelchair.*] Do you see those hopscotch squares on the floor? Would you be so good as to hop through them in the traditional way? You can choose which leg you favor.

HUMBLE
[*With scathing disdain.*] I thought you were interested in the quality of my thinking.

INTERVIEWER 2
Oh, we are, we are. We're also interested in your work ethic and ability to follow guidelines—and your spirit of play—to find meaning in what others might miss. Isn't that what numbers men do? They find significance in small amounts and little details. That's the principle that many of the most successful white-collar thieves practice. Big amounts raise eyebrows…but small amounts over time…

HUMBLE
What are you inferring?

INTERVIEWER 2
You mean implying. You were inferring. I wasn't implying anything. There's also the basic matter of coordination, balance and general fitness. The company offers a generous and comprehensive medical plan…as you can see. But we like to know at the outset a few things. I'm sure the urine test won't bother you either.

HUMBLE
Urine?

INTERVIEWER 2
Many companies now are requiring DNA, fingerprints and intensive diagnostic testing. Haven't you been keeping up to date? Perhaps because you were in business for yourself, you were able to scoot around best practice standards.

HUMBLE
I didn't scoot around anything.

INTERVIEWER 2
Well, you didn't keep in touch with the requirements your clients were forced to meet.

HUMBLE
I was busy watching their money.

INTERVIEWER 2
Indeed. Now hop along please.

[THE HUMBLE ASSESSMENT]

[HUMBLE *reluctantly hops through the squares.*]

INTERVIEWER 2
And back.

[HUMBLE *hops back.*]

INTERVIEWER 2
Fine. Here's the urine sample jar. [*Hands him the Erlenmeyer flask.*]

HUMBLE
You want me—you want me to piss right here?

INTERVIEWER 2
You can turn around if you like.

HUMBLE
You can't be…

INTERVIEWER 2
The faster you work with us, the sooner you may work for us.

[HUMBLE *shuffles off to a dark corner and turns his back. We hear fluid tinkle in the container. When he turns back and returns it to the desk, the amount of course looks very small given the size of the flask.*]

INTERVIEWER 2
Now we're going to do a simple verbal association test. You know how these work right? I say a word and then you tell me the first thing that pops into your mind. Try to keep your answers to one word. No thinking about it, no muddling it over. It's just what occurs to you, OK? Are you ready?

HUMBLE
Why not?

INTERVIEWER 2
Flee.

HUMBLE
Do you mean the insect, or to...?

INTERVIEWER 2
To what?

HUMBLE
Well, if you mean the insect, I'd say circus. If you mean the...

INTERVIEWER 2
Verb?

HUMBLE
I'd say run.

INTERVIEWER 2
Let's start again. Fly.

HUMBLE
You mean the insect or to...

INTERVIEWER 2
[*Takes pens from holder and writes in ledger.*] Often thinks of insects.

HUMBLE
I just mean if it was a housefly I'd say swatter. And if it was like to fly, I'd say airplane.

INTERVIEWER 2
Let's start yet again. [*Replaces pen.*] Humble. [HUMBLE *doesn't respond.*] "Humble" is the word.

HUMBLE
Pie.

INTERVIEWER 2
Pie. "Pie."

HUMBLE
Slice.

INTERVIEWER 2
Hammer.

HUMBLE
Nail.

INTERVIEWER 2
Very good. I think you're getting the hang of it. Let's see if we can pick up the pace, shall we? Nail.

HUMBLE
Hammer…

INTERVIEWER 2
Coffin.

HUMBLE
Nail.

INTERVIEWER 2
Beautiful.

HUMBLE
Lovely.

INTERVIEWER 2
Wretched.

HUMBLE
Poor.

INTERVIEWER 2
Lucky.

HUMBLE
Rich.

INTERVIEWER 2
Cushion.

HUMBLE
Pin.

INTERVIEWER 2
Pin.

HUMBLE
Needle.

INTERVIEWER 2
Fist.

HUMBLE
Glove.

INTERVIEWER 2
Water.

HUMBLE
Wine.

INTERVIEWER 2
Peach.

HUMBLE
Fuzz.

INTERVIEWER 2
Candy.

HUMBLE
Cotton.

INTERVIEWER 2
Sweet.

HUMBLE
Tooth.

INTERVIEWER 2
Snowman.

HUMBLE
Carrot.

INTERVIEWER 2
Interesting...Fortune.

HUMBLE
Cookie.

INTERVIEWER 2
Blank.

HUMBLE
Page.

INTERVIEWER 2
Monkey.

HUMBLE
Wrench.

INTERVIEWER 2
Banana.

HUMBLE
Monkey.

INTERVIEWER 2
Soldier.

HUMBLE
Army.

INTERVIEWER 2
Cream.

HUMBLE
Corn.

INTERVIEWER 2
Liar.

HUMBLE
Fire.

INTERVIEWER 2
Bent.

HUMBLE
Crooked.

INTERVIEWER 2
Wind.

HUMBLE
Leaves.

INTERVIEWER 2
Sharp.

HUMBLE
Pain.

INTERVIEWER 2
Window.

HUMBLE
Curtain.

INTERVIEWER 2
Dog.

[THE HUMBLE ASSESSMENT]

HUMBLE
Bone.

INTERVIEWER 2
Pregnant.

HUMBLE
Pause.

INTERVIEWER 2
[*Pauses.*] Lemon.

HUMBLE
Lime.

INTERVIEWER 2
Store.

HUMBLE
Save.

INTERVIEWER 2
That's optimistic.

HUMBLE
Store in a cool dry place.

INTERVIEWER 2
Pinch.

HUMBLE
Salt.

INTERVIEWER 2
Clam.

HUMBLE
Chowder.

INTERVIEWER 2
Victim.

HUMBLE
Crime.

INTERVIEWER 2
Wash.

HUMBLE
Hands.

INTERVIEWER 2
Fun.

HUMBLE
Game.

INTERVIEWER 2
Game.

HUMBLE
Sport.

INTERVIEWER 2
Sport.

HUMBLE
Hunting.

INTERVIEWER 2
Wagon.

HUMBLE
Rut.

INTERVIEWER 2
Trapeze.

HUMBLE
Net.

INTERVIEWER 2
Pigeon.

HUMBLE
Hole.

INTERVIEWER 2
Mouse.

HUMBLE
Trap.

INTERVIEWER 2
Pickle.

HUMBLE
Baseball.

INTERVIEWER 2
Baseball?

HUMBLE
I coached Little League once.

INTERVIEWER 2
Final one—Hasenpfeffer.

HUMBLE
Bugs.

INTERVIEWER 2
Back to insects?

HUMBLE
Bugs Bunny. I don't know what hasenpfeffer is. Some kind of rabbit stew. It was in a Bugs Bunny cartoon.

INTERVIEWER 2
Really...

HUMBLE
Yosemite Sam was in it.

INTERVIEWER 2
Do you find that strange?

HUMBLE
What?

INTERVIEWER 2
That you'd remember a Bugs Bunny cartoon?

HUMBLE
No.

INTERVIEWER 2
You don't find that at all odd that a man your age applying for a position like this would recall a Bugs Bunny cartoon?

HUMBLE
I didn't think about it. It just came to me. Isn't that the point?

INTERVIEWER 2
The point?

HUMBLE
Actually, I think that was a cartoon too. Harry Nilsson wrote the music.

INTERVIEWER 2
Tell me about Harry Nilsson.

HUMBLE
He's dead. He did a song called "All By Myself."

INTERVIEWER 2
Do you often feel that way?

HUMBLE
Dead?

INTERVIEWER 2
All by yourself.

HUMBLE
No more than most.

INTERVIEWER 2
You're sure of that?

HUMBLE
I haven't really thought about it. How would you know what others feel?

INTERVIEWER 2
Indeed. Indeed. [*Takes pen from holder.*]

HUMBLE
What are you writing now?

INTERVIEWER 2
Just another note for your file. [*Replaces pen.*] Shall we try some general knowledge questions? [*Reaches down and pulls what appears to be a playing card from the top hat.*]

Who said, "If you can't stand the heat, stay out of the kitchen?"

HUMBLE
Harry Truman.

INTERVIEWER 2
[*He flings the card away and pulls another from the hat.*] What's the speed of light?

HUMBLE
I've forgotten. I know it takes light from the sun about eight minutes or so to reach us, and the sun's 93 million miles away. So, like about 180,000 miles or more per second.

INTERVIEWER 2
186,000. Not bad. [*Tosses card and pulls another one from the hat.*] Where would you expect to find a wildebeest?

HUMBLE
On television.

INTERVIEWER 2
Clever. [*Pulls another card from the hat.*] Which freezes faster, tap water or boiling water?

HUMBLE
Boiling water. It has to do with the molecules moving around. I read that.

INTERVIEWER 2
How many legs are there on an elephant?

HUMBLE
A normal elephant?

INTERVIEWER 2
Yes, for the purposes of this discussion, let's grant that the elephant is healthy and normal in every way. In other words, it's not a mutation or hasn't been mutilated in some horrific tragedy.

HUMBLE
Four.

INTERVIEWER 2
How many legs on a spider?

HUMBLE
Like your tarantula? Eight.

INTERVIEWER 2
How many sides to a circle?

HUMBLE
Two. Inside and out.

[THE HUMBLE ASSESSMENT]

INTERVIEWER 2
Is there a relationship between 2, 4 and 8?

HUMBLE
Four and eight are multiples of 2. 2 squared is 4, 2 cubed is 8.

INTERVIEWER 2
Numbers man. If two cars are coming towards each other at 60 miles per hour and have a head-on collision, what's the level of impact.

HUMBLE
[*His voice drops.*] A hundred and twenty miles per hour.

INTERVIEWER 2
Numbers man. And if one car is going 85 miles per hour?

HUMBLE
One hundred and forty five miles…per hour.

INTERVIEWER 2
What's your favorite girl's name?

HUMBLE
That doesn't seem like a general knowledge question.

INTERVIEWER 2
Humor me.

HUMBLE
I don't have one.

INTERVIEWER 2
Elizabeth? Diane. Emily. Sarah?

HUMBLE
I don't have one.

INTERVIEWER 2
Tell me about your childhood. You had one of those, right?

HUMBLE
What does that have to do with the job?

INTERVIEWER 2
Well, since you ask…one theory of job satisfaction states that people are happiest and most productive when they're doing something that links back to childhood aptitudes and inclinations. When did you first realize you wanted to be a financial controller?

HUMBLE
When did you first realize this is what you wanted to do? Insulting people, playing head games with them. Humiliating them. Raking them over the coals.

INTERVIEWER 2
Is that what you feel is being done to you? You're being raked over coals?

HUMBLE
You heard what I said.

INTERVIEWER 2
What was your favorite chocolate bar as a kid? I don't seem to have that information.

HUMBLE
3 Musketeers.

INTERVIEWER 2
Interesting. I'd had you pegged for Snickers. Breakfast cereal?

HUMBLE
Post Toasties.

INTERVIEWER 2
You see? It's all coming back. Did you have a dog?

HUMBLE
A labradoodle named Slider. It ran away.

[THE HUMBLE ASSESSMENT]

INTERVIEWER 2
And?

HUMBLE
You want to know about my childhood? I got beaten up in school. Then I beat up another kid and never got beaten up again. My father was a dentist. He hated his job but he did it well. He didn't drink or smoke. He'd wanted to be a doctor but his grades weren't good enough. He liked doctor shows like *Marcus Welby, MD*. He liked to wax his car. Our first car was a Plymouth. Then he bought a Buick Electra. We lived in a nice house.

INTERVIEWER 2
What kind of house?

HUMBLE
A nice house.

INTERVIEWER 2
Describe it.

HUMBLE
A rose-colored house on Mock Orange Lane. Split level. I had a friend named Skip who could talk like Donald Duck. My sister was overweight. Until she became anorexic. She lives in Cincinnati now and is unhappily married—to a dentist. They live in a very nice house. I used to ride my bike down by the warehouses. Then one day an old man came after me. I didn't ride down there any more. I was always a solid B student, but I did well in math. I became an accountant because I wanted to live in a nice house. I started off in private practice, and then got headhunted by my major client. I left that job because I thought I could make more money on my own, but it's hard being in business for yourself these days. How's that for honesty?

INTERVIEWER 2
Astounding.

HUMBLE
You making fun of me again? I haven't had an interesting life. You

don't want someone interesting as financial controller.

INTERVIEWER 2
What about your mother?

HUMBLE
What about her? She died of Hodgkins when I was sixteen.

INTERVIEWER 2
You don't think that's interesting?

HUMBLE
I think it's sad.

INTERVIEWER 2
She died when you were sixteen? Or when you turned sixteen?

HUMBLE
Yeah. She died on my birthday. OK? [*Pause.*] How did you know that?

INTERVIEWER 2
What else happened on that day?

HUMBLE
How did you know that?

INTERVIEWER 2
What else happened on that day?

HUMBLE
I—lost my virginity.

INTERVIEWER 2
You don't think that's interesting?

HUMBLE
I…

INTERVIEWER 2
Did you see your mother before she died? That day?

HUMBLE
No...

INTERVIEWER 2
Why didn't you see her?

HUMBLE
Because...

INTERVIEWER 2
Because you were with Lauren Kennedy. Little Lauren, who you watched *Born Free* with. She had pigtails. Then she got big boobs.

HUMBLE
How did you know that? What's going on?

INTERVIEWER 2
Didn't you say, you're being raked over the coals?

HUMBLE
But—

INTERVIEWER 2
Now put on the helmet there and take the I Test.

HUMBLE
What?

INTERVIEWER 2
PUT ON THE HELMET!

HUMBLE
All...right...I... [HUMBLE *puts on the welder's helmet.*] I can't see. [*He gropes for the security of the desk.*]

INTERVIEWER 2
What did you think you'd be able to see?

HUMBLE
You said...

INTERVIEWER 2
I said I Test. As in me. You. As in memory and connection with life. There are many different ways of seeing, and therefore many different kinds of blindness. All you have to do to pass this test is to describe me. As precisely as you can. That should be easy.

HUMBLE
I...

INTERVIEWER 2
C'mon. What do I look like?

HUMBLE
I...

INTERVIEWER 2
What was your mother's name?

HUMBLE
Hel-en.

INTERVIEWER 2
Helen. The face that launched a thousand ships. What was your wife's name?

HUMBLE
Helen.

INTERVIEWER 2
You don't find that interesting? Now tell me what I look like. Where's the trick in that? Just tell the audience in simple terms what I look like.

HUMBLE
I...

INTERVIEWER 2
What color are my eyes?

HUMBLE
I...

INTERVIEWER 2
You know there's an audience watching don't you? They've been here the whole time. Watching you. There's always been an audience watching. Watching you spit on the old man down by the warehouses. Do you know why he ran up to you? Yes, he was a little crazy, and maybe you should've been scared of him. But you'd seen him before plenty of times, and he'd seen you. He just came up to you because his cat was having kittens. He was excited. He chose you to share that moment with. He wanted to know if you wanted a kitten. And you didn't just ride off did you? You spat on him.

HUMBLE
I...

INTERVIEWER 2
One little good moment in that old man's life.

HUMBLE
I...

INTERVIEWER 2
He didn't live in a nice house, did he? He lived in a shack in the blackberries by Oriole Creek. You never did see an oriole there did you? Just flat tires and empty cans of Mountain Dew.

HUMBLE
I...

INTERVIEWER 2
The old man died not long after that, didn't he?

HUMBLE
I...

INTERVIEWER 2
You made up a story to impress your friends. You said the cat and the kittens started eating his dead body. You said they ate out his eyes.

HUMBLE
I...

INTERVIEWER 2
You can see the audience now, can't you? You can't see anything else, but you can see them. The audience that's always been there. Like your friend Skip. He was the one you beat up, didn't you? So you wouldn't be all by yourself.

HUMBLE
I...

INTERVIEWER 2
And your sister, who in fact became bulimic and almost died because...because of what?

HUMBLE
I...

INTERVIEWER 2
Because you tormented her about her eating. Her weight. What was your special nickname for her. The one you taunted her with? Ah, yes. Macaroon. Cute. What's her real name?

HUMBLE
M-mi...

INTERVIEWER 2
What was your daughter's name?

HUMBLE
M-mi...

INTERVIEWER 2
Do you have a speech impediment? You should've advised us.

HUMBLE
M-mi...

INTERVIEWER 2
You named your only daughter after your sister—who you raked over the coals as you put it.

HUMBLE
Mi-a. Mia.

INTERVIEWER 2
And methinks culpa. Why did you neglect to mention that she also died in the car accident that claimed your wife Helen's life?

HUMBLE
I...

INTERVIEWER 2
Why didn't you say that you were driving?

HUMBLE
I...

INTERVIEWER 2
Why didn't you say you were driving?

HUMBLE
I...

INTERVIEWER 2
How old was your daughter when she died?

HUMBLE
Six-teen...

INTERVIEWER 2
Sixteen. How fast were you driving?

HUMBLE
Eight—eighty-five. Miles per hour.

INTERVIEWER 2
Why were you driving so fast with your wife and daughter in the car?

HUMBLE
I…

INTERVIEWER 2
Did it have to do with your nice house, your job…the woman you were seeing—or all of the above?

HUMBLE
I…

INTERVIEWER 2
What was your woman on the side's name?

HUMBLE
Laur…en.

INTERVIEWER 2
You don't find that interesting?

HUMBLE
I…

INTERVIEWER 2
She was 43 then wasn't she? You were surprised when she told you she was pregnant.

HUMBLE
I…

INTERVIEWER 2
Must've been awkward.

HUMBLE
I...

INTERVIEWER 2
She was going to spoil everything for you, if she blew the whistle on you, wasn't she?

HUMBLE
I...

INTERVIEWER 2
She wanted money. So, you worked out a way to dip into the till, didn't you?

HUMBLE
I...

INTERVIEWER 2
Just a little bit...in a way you knew you could cover. But she wanted more, right?

HUMBLE
More...

INTERVIEWER 2
And she found out from you how to take it. You'd have lost your contract if you hadn't gone along with her.

HUMBLE
Lost...

INTERVIEWER 2
She could've gotten you terminated and exposed you to your wife. You'd have been picked clean in a divorce settlement. She played you like a horn.

HUMBLE
Played me...

INTERVIEWER 2
You don't even know if she was really pregnant. She used you.

HUMBLE
Used me…

INTERVIEWER 2
She used your skill as a numbers man to bilk quite a bit of money, didn't she? The kind of money you couldn't cover up.

HUMBLE
Cover up…

INTERVIEWER 2
Then she conveniently disappeared that day of the city train crash. Never heard from again. As if she'd planned the whole thing. It's funny how things work out, isn't it?

HUMBLE
Funny…

INTERVIEWER 2
And then the terrible car accident. What really happened?

HUMBLE
I…don't…know…

INTERVIEWER 2
Isn't it interesting that your car accident and the train wreck happened on the same day?

HUMBLE
I…don't…know…

INTERVIEWER 2
Take off the helmet and look at me. What color are my eyes?

HUMBLE
I…I don't…know…

INTERVIEWER 2
What's in the bowl?

HUMBLE
Noth-ing.

INTERVIEWER 2
Oh, yes there is. There's something in the bowl, isn't there? [*Pause.*] Put your hand in it.

HUMBLE
N-no...

INTERVIEWER 2
Put your hand in it.

HUMBLE
Pl-ease. No...

INTERVIEWER 2
Put your hand in it.

HUMBLE
[*Against his will, he reaches out and puts his hand in the empty jar and bellows as if in agony.*] AAAHHHHHHHH!!!!

INTERVIEWER 2
[*Five beat silence.*] You can go now. You know the way. You know the way so well.

HUMBLE
I...[*Takes off the helmet at last and drops it on the floor, utterly spent.*]

INTERVIEWER 2
We'll see you next time.

[HUMBLE *staggers off into the shadows, shattered. The second* INTERVIEWER *makes a final note in the ledger and then slaps it shut. The lights begin to fade, and the wheelchair turns. Before all goes dark we think we catch just a glimpse of the* INTERVIEWER'S *face. We can't be sure but it seems as if the eye sockets are sealed over and blank. Blackout.*]

EPILOGUE

INTERVIEWER 1 *sits at a three-quarter angle with her back to us. This time she is completely topless. A large steel dog cage waits on the floor with its door open.*

Everything else on the desk is as before.

On the floor beside the cage is a gigantic brightly colored beach ball.

[HUMBLE *wanders in vaguely out of the dark, clutching a huge stuffed animal, which he absently drops on the floor the moment he passes out of the shadows into the light. The light seems especially harsh on him when he finally sits down.*]

INTERVIEWER 1
Come in, Mr. Crumble.

HUMBLE
Humble.

INTERVIEWER 1
You're humble? Well, don't be shy too. Take a seat.

HUMBLE
I'm *a* Humble. [*He looks at the cage and then goes to sit down precariously on the beach ball.*]

INTERVIEWER 1
A humble what?

HUMBLE
That's my name. Richard Humble. Didn't you—

INTERVIEWER 1
I'm sorry about that.

HUMBLE
[*Smiles.*] Are you…making fun?

INTERVIEWER 1
Why? I'm sure plenty of others have done that.

HUMBLE
[*Now a bit miffed.*] I haven't gotten *your* name…the girl on the desk—

INTERVIEWER 1
No, you got a rather silly name. But I'll just call you 16.

[THE HUMBLE ASSESSMENT]

HUMBLE
16? You've done 15 interviews for this position?

INTERVIEWER 1
Why would you think that?

HUMBLE
Because you just said 16...

INTERVIEWER 1
That's only because it's an easy number for me to remember. Are you trying to work out the odds—what your chances are?

HUMBLE
Well, I'd like...

INTERVIEWER 1
Given your age—and from what I know of actuarial tables—I'm not sure you'd like to know the odds of you even still being alive.

HUMBLE
Now wait a...

[*A terrible, hideous scream of pure anguish erupts offstage.*]

HUMBLE
What was THAT?

INTERVIEWER 1
Oh, just a training session in progress. Team building exercises.

HUMBLE
T-team...?

INTERVIEWER 1
You look very tired. Did you walk all the way in again?

HUMBLE
I...

INTERVIEWER 1
I bet you're hungry too. I've got some nice lively crickets for you.

[*Behind* HUMBLE, *a screen illuminates and we see projected once more the tarantula being fed crickets. The stage gradually goes dark until only the spider remains...then it too fades.*]

THE THEATER OF AMBUSH:
AN AFTERWORD

"Theoretically, it should be possible to 'peel' the collective unconsciousness, layer by layer, until we come to the psychology of the worm, even the amoeba."

—Carl S. Jung

"...in the animal, man, there still functions a worm."

—Wilhelm Reich

I grew up surrounded by theater. The First Congregational Church my parents ran seemed highly theatrical to my young eyes, with people in robes, strange moments of silent prayer, and then grand singing...stained glass windows...the brightly colored ceremonial fabrics. There's a great deal of both subtle and highly explicit theater in the ritual of many kinds of church services.

Then more literally, as choir director of my father's church, my mother was always conducting pageants and performances of some kind, to keep us Sunday Schoolers engaged. She received a Master's in Dramatic Arts from Cal Berkeley, and when she became the drama teacher at King Junior High School in Oakland, it seemed I spent a lot of my early childhood years wandering around backstage amidst the crude school shop-made fragments of hopeful magic we call props… a Styrofoam dragon's tail spray painted a lurid green…a tinfoil knight's wooden broadsword… cardboard gravestones…even a paper moon. I was fascinated and deeply moved.

As I was by the words emerging out of the stage lights, reaching out into the dark. Whether it was two kids up on ladders from a scene from *Our Town*, or the Jury of the Dead coming forth from *The Devil and Daniel Webster*, there's something fundamentally powerful about language performed live. I think no matter how hokey and please-the-parents school plays and summer camp skits may be, there's still that link back to the dreams and visions of very long ago. For it could well be that "Theater" in its natural inclusiveness of comedy, drama, education, visual art, music, dance, poetry and song, is the oldest art form of all—the river source of all the sub-specialties.

The first play I ever wrote was called *The Abombinable Snowman?*—an extended sketch for my sixth grade class, performed by me, and my friends Noel, Kim, Jorge and Butler. Not surprisingly, it had to do with a climbing party lost in a snowstorm in the mountains of Nepal/Tibet. Jorge, a fiercely dark and newly arrived kid from Mexico, played the Snowman (by his own insistence) and wore what we would call today a white hoodie and some toy sunglasses with extra large white frames (when I think about that today, it seems very hip and lateral). There wasn't much to the plot, as you can imagine—certainly nothing original. The arrogance of the climbers gets them hopelessly lost, then the resident monster, which they at first don't believe in, and then want to attack, actually ends up saving their lives. What I am proud of though is that I managed to work in the one kid in the whole class who hadn't been cast in any other of the skits. Jeff Crowe wasn't used to not being picked, because he was a very good athlete and a pretty tough fighter in the pine trees behind the school. But in the classroom, he really struggled. He had both a very bad stammer and a reading problem—and a temper that made both worse. What part could be play? Unlike Jorge, who could bound around with slapstick grace, Jeff froze up the moment he was indoors. Dancing indoors paralyzed him to the same degree of intensity that a fight on the playground or a football game brought him to life. So, I hit on what to this day I think is a fine solution. He became a very special character, which added greatly to the mood of the piece—he was the Voice of the Howling Wind. Along with Jorge's acrobatic Snowman, he was the best part honestly. I'm still pondering the lesson of that all these years later: how what can be the most important element may not be on the page. It's easy to see why this is true in the world of theater and film—the script is not the performance. But mysteriously, I believe this lesson applies to not only all forms of writing, but all art in some way. I know this puzzles many people. They honestly go in search of art, and the better it is, the more elusive it seems.

My mother made a lot of potentially interesting dramatic experiences possible in my junior high school years. The trouble is we're so self-conscious at that time in life. There was one improv course run by a local regional theater that might've had a lot to offer—except I was the only male in the class, which is not a good look at that age. Nevertheless, I kept performing in school plays, and I was fortunate to have a drama teacher in high school, who was also one of the assistant football coaches and the head baseball coach. He brought a masculine aura of cool to the theater.

But what I really wanted to do wasn't recite other people's lines so much, I wanted to write my own. I won a host of writing prizes in the Scholastic Magazine Award competition, including the overall Best Entry Prize for a one-act play called *The Vivarium*, which was about two old women, modeled on my grandmother and great aunt, languishing in a suspect nursing home. I received $100 (which seemed a lot back then) and a Smith-Corona typewriter with a gold plate with my name on it. It was a hugely inspiring validation.

A class in Modern Drama opened me to the major Europeans: Chekhov, Ibsen, Strindberg (who I have a particular affinity with on many levels)...and that decisive psychotectonic shift wrought by Beckett, Ionesco, Pirandello, Giraudoux, Sartre—and the highly underrated Ugo Betti (if you aren't familiar with his *Crime on Goat Island*, I highly recommend it).

Although I didn't necessarily verbalize this all that articulately at the time, I was trying to come to terms with an artistic crisis—the schism between the poetic-symbolic, essentially realist tradition of the American theater (O'Neill, Wilder, Williams, Miller and Inge) and the more expressionistic and lyrically brutal work emerging through the European and avant-garde influences. Edward Albee's *The Zoo Story* blew me away (I still admire it). I have a great deal of respect for the work of Sam Shepard (especially the early wild pieces). But I was particularly intrigued by Harold Pinter, and his sense of menace and ambiguity. I have a profound admiration to this day for his observation that, "So often, below the word spoken, is the thing known and unspoken."

I'd go on to have many experiences with the theater. I played the Laurence Olivier part in *Sleuth* in high school. I met my oldest and dearest friend at ISOMATA, a summer camp for the arts run by USC in the mountains above Palm Springs. My mother took me to see a world premier of one of Tennessee Williams' late plays at ACT in San Francisco, and we literally ran into him personally after the show—one of the highlights of my life. Years later, in Australia, I even organized my own experimental guerilla troupe, complete with night fire effigies, masks, pirated equipment, cannibalized machines and industrial noise. I looked to such sources as Greek drama, Noh theater, Cantonese opera, Grand Guignol, marionette performance, religious festivals and mystery plays.

But I never had the skills or the resources to bring the sense of circus I craved to my chief interest—the dark use of language as weapon. I wanted the psychology of confrontation, and to peel back the layers of psychology to find the inner worm inside us. I don't say by any means that I have achieved that here, or that I will ever achieve it. But I like the notion of interrogating the idea anyway. *Interrogation* is a word I use a lot. When I was young, and on the surface a good student, I had the strange experience of being interrogated by the FBI in regards to my stepbrother's criminal activities. It was formative. I was later detained, deposed, questioned and outright beaten by various law enforcement bodies for various alleged misdoings. We've all faced the combat of the job interview, and I've always had a fixation on the process of the psychiatric evaluation. So, something of all this past boils over here in what you have in your hands. I'd like to believe it offers some interest. It's the first play I've written in twenty years, but I hope it won't be my last.

I think there's a case to be made that the complex shifting sands between Modernism and Postmodernism, at least in the literary arts, were navigated most interestingly and expressively by dramatists.

All the world's a stage is a line of poetry—but it was delivered

[THE THEATER OF AMBUSH: AN AFTERWORD]

from a stage, as its author intended. He didn't say the world's a poem, a story, or a piece of music. Shakespeare forcefully asserts that the world is theater. I may occasionally view it as some vast theme park or uncontrolled experiment—but a part of me will always agree with his assessment: *Theater*. Somehow, it seemed time to return to that cave of shadows and voices—of worms and ambiguities—of ambush and interrogation. Of things almost said, and then known all too well.

—Kris Saknussemm
Las Vegas, Nevada

KRIS SAKNUSSEMM is the internationally acclaimed author of the books *Zanesville*, *Private Midnight*, *Enigmatic Pilot*, *Reverend America*, *Sea Monkeys*, and the portfolio art books *The Colors of Compulsion* and *Possible Languages*. Lazy Fascist Press brought out a collection of his early short stories entitled *Sinister Miniatures*.

A native of the Bay Area in California, he is a graduate of Dartmouth College and the University of Washington, and attended the American Academy of Dramatic Arts in Pasadena. His dramatic works have been presented on ABC Radio National in Australia and in a live theater context in Melbourne, Sydney and New Zealand. His piece *Memory Wound* won the First Prize in the 10-Minute Play Competition for *The Missouri Review*.

www.ingramcontent.com/pod-product-compliance
Lightning Source LLC
LaVergne TN
LVHW041547070426
835507LV00011B/973